D1741895

# ADVENTURERS

## *SKIING*

### *Jeremy Evans*

**HEINEMANN**

First published by Heinemann Children's Reference 1992,
a division of Heinemann Educational Books Ltd, Halley Court,
Jordan Hill, Oxford OX2 8EJ

OXFORD LONDON EDINBURGH
MADRID PARIS ATHENS BOLOGNA
MELBOURNE SYDNEY AUCKLAND SINGAPORE
TOKYO IBADAN NAIROBI GABORONE HARARE
PORTSMOUTH (USA)

Design by Julian Holland Publishing Ltd

Printed in Hong Kong

**British Library Cataloguing in Publication Data**
Evans, Jeremy
  Skiing. – (Adventurers)
  I. Title II. Series
  796.93

ISBN 0-431-00593-1

**Acknowledgements**
Illustrations: Rupert White Studio, Martin Smillie, Keith Chaffer.
Photographs: a = above, m = middle, b = below
All photographs were taken by the author except;
Cover, Phoenix/Jess Stock; title page, Phoenix/Jess Stock; 4a, Courcheval Tourist Office; 5a Ski
Club; 6a, Courcheval Tourist Office; 8a, S. Chappaz; 10b, S. Chappaz; 13a, Rossignol; 14a,
Courcheval Tourist Office; 15b, Plas y Brenin; 21a, Rossignol; 22a, BASI; 26a, French
Government Tourist Office; 27b, BASI; 29a, Murren Tourist Office; 30a, Europa Sport/Mats
Lindgren; 32a, Courcheval Tourist Office; 33a, Rossignol; 34a, French Government Tourist
Office; 34b, French Government Tourist Office; 35a, Murren Tourist Office; 37a, Ski Club; 39a,
Rossignol; 39b, Blizzard; 40a, Rossignol; 41m, Les Arcs Tourist Office; 43a, Rossignol; 42b,
Nitro/Ron Dahlquist; 44a, Les Arcs Tourist Office; 45b, Fleet PR/David Brownell.

Thanks go to the following for their help: The British Ski Federation, Ski Club of Great Britain,
British Association of Ski Instructors, Ken Way of Ultrasport (Rossignol), Kate Bradford of Grange
International (Blizzard), Phoenix, Fleet PR, French Government Tourist Office, and the tourist
offices of Les Arcs, Courcheval, Megeve, and Murren.

**Note to the reader**
In this book there are some words in the text which are printed in **bold** type. This
shows that the word is listed in the glossary on page 46. The glossary gives a brief
explanation of words which may be new to you.

# Contents

# Time to ski

The ski season begins in winter when the snows start to fall over the mountains. The main centres in the northern hemisphere are in the Alps, Pyrenees and Rocky Mountains. In Europe and North America the season starts just before Christmas and finishes around Easter, while in the southern hemisphere the season is June to September. To enjoy skiing properly there must not only be snow but lots of it, and it should remain in tip-top condition if you are to get the best out of the sport. Usually the higher the ski resort is the better the snow will be. The height of resorts ranges from 600 metres above sea level to well over 2000. In the higher resorts it stays colder longer, keeping the snow frozen and postponing the day when it turns to slush and melts away. 'Go high' is good advice.

## The pioneers

Skiing started because people found that using skis was an easier and quicker way to get around on snow than walking. The earliest skis ever, dated around 2500BC, were found in Scandinavia. During the 19th century they were well known and much used in Northern Europe, the US, and in the Snowy Mountains of Australia. By the early years of the 20th century skiing had turned into a sport for rich European gentlemen, with the first ski schools established in Austria and Switzerland. In those days skiers had to climb their way up the snow covered slopes. Then in the 1930s the first **ski lifts,** designed to haul skiers up the slopes, appeared.

# Ski resorts

There are now over 3000 ski resorts worldwide, and they form a large part of the winter tourist business. The traditional resorts, such as Wengen and Zurich in Switzerland, have grown from pretty Alpine villages in beautiful surroundings, while the more modern style, such as Tignes and Isola 2000 in France, have been purpose-built as ski resorts. Thousands of ski enthusiasts will use them for one or two weeks a year.

Most of the **downhill skiing** in the resorts is done **on piste**, which means on specially prepared snow trails which are groomed, flattened and looked after by specially designed caterpillar track snowmobiles. Skiers are ferried to the top of the piste by various kinds of lifts, allowing them to ski down and then take the lift up again.

# The nursery slopes

For less experienced skiers and beginners the day usually starts on the gentlest slopes at the resort. These are called nursery slopes and here the local ski school holds its classes. These classes generally last a couple of hours in the morning, with a break for lunch before more skiing in the afternoon.

Skiing is hungry and thirsty work, and there's nothing better than sitting down to eat in a mountain restaurant. The ski lifts stop at around 4pm to give everyone plenty of time to get down off the mountain.

# Ski questions

**Q:** What is the difference between skiing 'on piste' and '**off piste**'?
**A.** Skiing on piste is on specially prepared trails. Off piste means going off the trail, often on **virgin powder snow**. The photograph shows the challenge of going off piste where the skier faces the elements with only skill to protect him.

# What to wear

Most people wear special clothes for skiing as they have to be warm, dry and comfortable. You need to be able to move freely for skiing and walking but must have clothing which can cope with extremes of temperature. You should wear layers that can be peeled off, but which will keep you dry if you fall into wet snow.

Skiing is by its nature a cold weather sport, but the amount of cold experienced can vary from possible danger of frostbite, to skiing comfortably in a T-shirt. In the northern hemisphere January and February are the coldest months while March and April can be comparatively warm. South of the equator June and July are coldest.

Many people like to pay attention to the new season's styles, so ski clothing is very fashion conscious.

## Safety first

● Dress for the cold. Wear enough layers to stay warm and dry. Protect your hands with gloves or mittens and your head with a woolly hat.
● Protect your eyes against glare. In extreme cases skiing with unprotected eyes can result in temporary **snow blindness.** Sunglasses will usually do, but wear goggles if it's snowing.
● Protect your skin against the sun. It may be cold, but on a fine day at high altitude the sun has a very powerful effect. Always protect your face with a **sun block**.

# Special clothing

For really cold weather and for skiing through deep powder snow a one-piece ski suit may be best. The disadvantage of a one-piece is that you can't peel off layers to cool down if the weather warms up. Most skiers prefer the greater freedom offered by **salopettes.** These are trousers cut chest-high with braces, rather like dungarees. They can be worn together with a short wind and waterproof jacket. The favourite style of shirt is a **sous-pull** or cotton zippered polo neck. This allows you to unzip the neck and roll up your sleeves if you get too hot. In the coldest weather you will also need extra layers such as pullovers and thermal underwear, including long johns if necessary. Special ski socks with fluffy insides and smooth outsides complete your basic clothing.

A woolly hat or balaclava prevents heat loss from the head.

Wear sunglasses or goggles to cut out glare from the snow. Your face should be protected by a sun block.

The best ski jackets are useful as well as fashionable. Bright colours combine with good warmth.

Ski trousers should keep you warm and dry. The bottoms should fit over your ski boots and have an elasticated cuff.

Mittens are warmer, but gloves are easier to use with ski poles. They must be waterproof.

Ski socks should come above the tops of the boots, to help prevent them rubbing.

# Choosing skis

The traditional way of choosing the right length skis used to be to see how high you could reach. Long skis give more support on soft snow and therefore go faster. They are always used for competition and other high performance skiing. However, due to their length they are much more difficult to turn than shorter skis. For this reason most beginners and intermediate skiers find it much easier to use skis which reach to around head height. If you are very light you can use short skis, but if you are heavier you will need skis that are a little longer to support your weight, especially on soft snow.

## Designed for efficiency

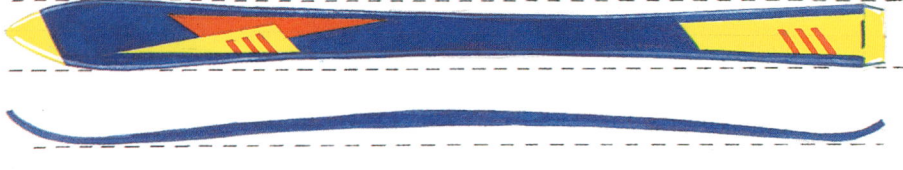

At first sight skis are straight sided and, apart from the turned up tips at the front, appear flat. If you look more closely though, you will see that they are widest at the front and cut in or 'waisted' at the sides, called **sidecut**. This is less obvious on short compact skis. The sidecut helps the ski to turn more easily when it's on its edge. On the bottom there is a narrow full length groove which helps straight running. When seen side-on skis are also turned up at the tails as well as at the tips. The curve from tip to tail is called the **camber**.

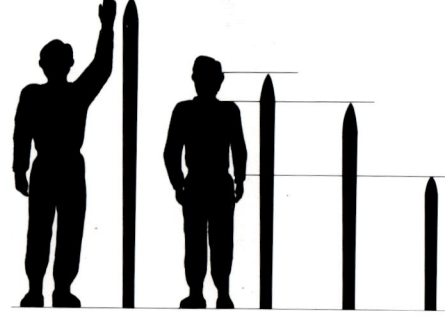

Long skis go faster, compact skis are more manoeuvrable, and very short skis are sometimes favoured for learning. A hire shop or ski school will advise you.

# What skis are made of

Skis were originally made of wood. Now they are built up from layers of materials glued or bonded together. This gives the right degree of stiffness, strength, and light weight. Most have a central wooden core which is the heart of the ski. This is reinforced by metal, rubber or fibreglass with a tough plastic outer skin made of **ABS** and polyethylene. The all-important sharp edges which allow the ski to grip on ice or snow are made of steel and must be kept in good condition.

# Buy or hire?

A top class pair of skis and boots is very expensive. If you outgrow them they become useless to you, and, added to this, skis usually need replacing or become outdated within three years. By comparison you can hire boots and skis at a resort for a reasonable charge, as well as get expert help and advice on what best suits you. Besides, it's hard work travelling by plane, train or car while lugging your own heavy boots and skis with you. So until you decide whether you are a serious skier or not there are strong reasons for hiring rather than buying.

# Care of equipment

If you don't keep moving, skis can freeze over and won't slide on fresh snow. Most experienced skiers carry a block of wax to give their skis a quick rub over. You can also use a spray-on wax solution.

Skis can get seriously damaged if they hit a rock or something equally hard. The usual upkeep involves waxing the bottoms and sharpening the edges of the skis. These steel edges must be kept sharp to give control on hard packed snow and ice. Ski shops and hire centres do this using a specialist type of machine. You can hand sharpen skis with a file, as shown in the photograph. All top competition skiers prefer to do this themselves. They say that it takes around two hours to sharpen the edges of one ski.

Waxing is very important to help protect the bottom or sole of the ski, and to keep it running freely on fresh snow. This is another specialist job best done by a shop. Hot, liquid wax is dropped onto the ski, and then an iron is used to spread it evenly over the surface. When set, most of the wax is then scraped from the bottom.

# Ski footwear

The main accessories that allow you to ski at all are all attached to your feet – the boots, the bindings, and the skis themselves. In the days before lifts skiers would use walking boots, which allowed them to walk up the hillsides before they attached the skis and skied back down. Now we use purpose-made ski boots which force your legs into a knees-bent position. They are so solid and supportive that when used with modern bindings, leg or ankle injuries are unlikely.

# Choosing your boots

Like skis and bindings, boots are extremely expensive to buy unless you ski regularly, and are best hired at a resort. They are made from a heavy outer plastic casing with a thick, foam-padded inner liner. Different styles include front entry and rear entry. Rear entry hinge open at the back and are generally easiest to get into. You must have ski boots that fit well. You should be able to move your toes, but otherwise your foot should be firmly and comfortably positioned with your heels held firmly down. At the same time the boots must be flexible enough so that you can push your shins forward to help control the skis. To allow for this most boots have some kind of hinge.

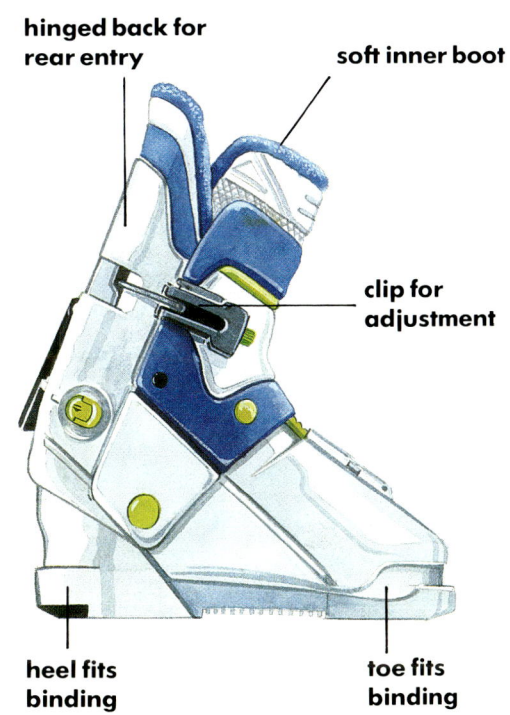

**hinged back for rear entry**

**soft inner boot**

**clip for adjustment**

**heel fits binding**

**toe fits binding**

# How bindings work

In earlier days the bindings which attached the boots to the skis used straps and laces. Nowadays they are wholly mechanical, but they keep the old name of bindings. The binding is part of the ski, and must be adjusted for a perfect fit with the boot. If you fall over, one or both bindings will immediately release the ski from the boot.

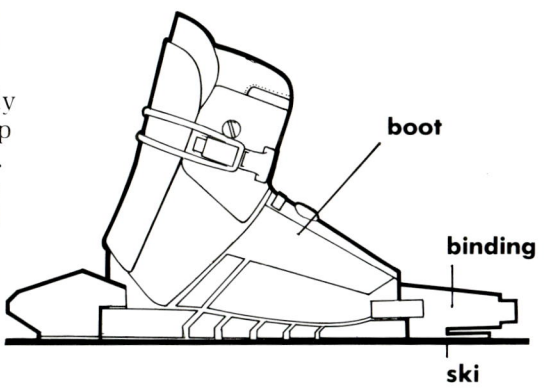

**boot**

**binding**

**ski**

## Wearing skis

When you are learning to ski, the skis are most easily put on when you're on flat ground. If you're on a hill you must place them across the slope, which is called the **fall line.** Always put the downhill one on first.

Remove all the snow you can from your boots and bindings before putting on your skis. If you don't, the **binding release system** may not work. Knock off snow with your ski poles, and place the toe of your boot in the front of the binding. Push down with your heel, and the back of the binding will automatically lock into place. This lifts the **ski stoppers** which are two little struts that stick down into the snow and prevent unsecured skis from running away downhill.

## Carrying correctly

To take off skis, you have to press the **release mechanism lever** at the back of the binding. If you are on a slope, start with the uphill ski first, using the tip of your ski pole to press the lever.

Skis should be carried with their bottoms together, using the ski stoppers to hold them parallel. They are quite heavy, and most skiers favour carrying them over their shoulder with tips down and tails up as shown. Take great care when turning that you don't hit someone with the tail end.

Your ski poles can be carried in the other hand, and used for balance. In a confined space, such as when travelling in a **gondola lift**, you will need to carry the skis upright with the tails down.

# Ski poles

You need ski poles for support and balance, though when you're learning the essential basic skills of balance and control it's often helpful to ski without them. They are made of light alloy with rubber hand grips, wrist straps, and pointed tips with plastic baskets which prevent the pole driving too far down into the snow. Most skiers use straight poles, but racers such as the one above favour bent poles which fit round the body for better aerodynamic performance.

The poles must be the right height. To check this in a hire shop or on hard ground, hold the pole upside down. Your forearm should be parallel to the ground when your hand holds the pole just under the basket. This means that when the tip is planted in the snow, your forearm will be at the same correct angle.

# Ski schools

Most resorts have official ski schools, run with the approval of a national authority. They cater for skiers of all ages and abilities, starting with kindergarten classes for three and four year olds. The schools are split into various classes, ranging upwards from Class 1 for beginners. A lesson will usually last around two hours, with a qualified instructor leading and teaching. Obviously the smaller the size of the class the more you are likely to learn. Ten pupils is about the most that a good instructor should be expected to handle. Most people sign up for a week of ski lessons – either two lessons a day or a lesson in the morning, with free skiing in the afternoon. Apart from learning, it's a good way to make new friends on the ski slopes.

## Progress through classes

The Swiss ski school system divides teaching into six classes:
CLASS 1 teaches you the basics of the nursery slopes including snowploughs. CLASS 2 takes you a little higher onto riding T-bars, traversing, and learning to sideslip. By CLASS 3 you are no longer a beginner, and are probably on your second skiing holiday. Turns develop to open parallel turning. CLASS 4 moves further into parallel skiing. CLASSES 5 and 6 are for expert skiers, learning advanced techniques, and off piste skiing.

# Using short skis

Very short skis are used for teaching in the French **Ski Evolutif** method which originated at the French resort of Les Arcs. It's now used at a number of resorts in Europe, and is called the Graduated Length Method in the US. The idea is that you start learning on very short skis. These stop just behind your boots, and unlike with ordinary compact skis, at first you are likely to fall flat on your back. As you get better you change to longer skis, and keep changing until you're on the full length skis.

Whether Ski Evolutif makes learning to ski easier is a matter of opinion. If you have a good instructor and are keen to learn you can make very fast progress the traditional way.

# Dry slopes

In countries where there is little or no snow, a favourite method of giving skiing a go is to try it on a dry ski slope as shown in the photograph. This is an artificial slope covered in plastic matting. While you can learn the basics of skiing, it does not give the same exhilaration as skiing on real snow. It is also harder and more unforgiving to fall on. If there's a **dry slope** in your area it's probably worth a visit before you go to the real thing, to give you a head start over other beginners. In fact skiers can become quite expert on dry slopes and then find snow much easier. Some skiers visit them frequently, taking part in dry slope racing competitions.

15

# On the piste

The prepared pistes of ski resorts are divided into different colour coded runs, and some resorts will also have off piste routes for expert skiers. All resorts have maps showing where the piste routes go. These are graded mainly according to how steep they are, with the easiest runs on the gentlest slopes. They are signposted to direct the skiers which way to go.

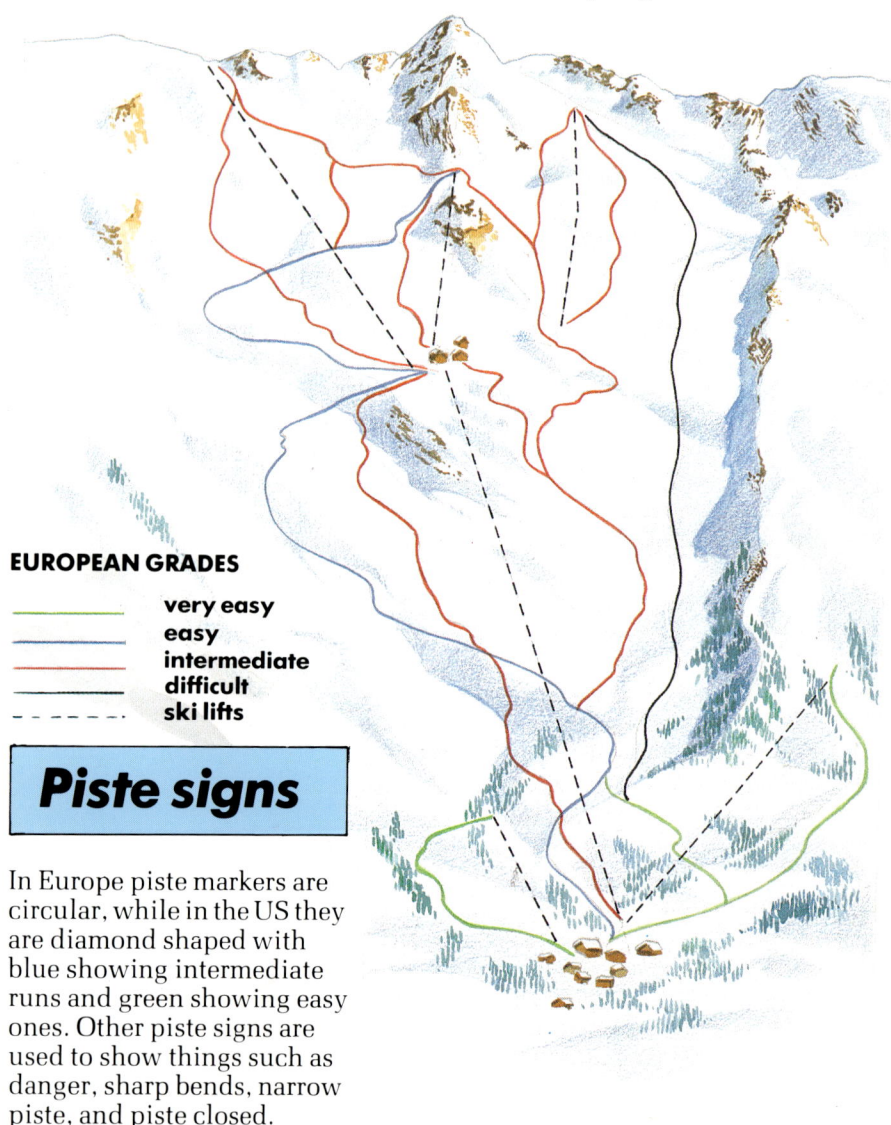

**EUROPEAN GRADES**

— **very easy**
— **easy**
— **intermediate**
— **difficult**
- - - - **ski lifts**

## Piste signs

In Europe piste markers are circular, while in the US they are diamond shaped with blue showing intermediate runs and green showing easy ones. Other piste signs are used to show things such as danger, sharp bends, narrow piste, and piste closed.

# Skiing safely

After a week of ski lessons, anyone with a good sporting background will probably be able to handle basic **parallel turning** and be able to ski down all green runs, most blue ones, and maybe some red ones if their nerve will stand it. If you fall into this group you should be able to take care of yourself on the piste, but remember that you owe it to yourself and to others to ski safely. Nowadays, most ski accidents are caused by collisions on the piste. Always look where you're going, look ahead so you can stop in plenty of time, and if the visibility is bad go slowly. Never attempt to ski beyond your ability. You should always be in reasonable control, rather than hurtling down some strange slope in the hope that there will be nothing unexpected round the corner.

## Rights of way

● The skier overtaking keeps clear. Remember that the other skier can't see you coming from behind, so if in doubt call out.
● When overtaking a skier on a **traverse**, overtake on the uphill side.
● Always overtake as widely as possible.
● It is the overtaker's responsibility to overtake on the more dangerous side.
● Only stop where skiers behind can see you in plenty of time, and where they have plenty of space to overtake.
● If you fall on a narrow piste, try to get out of the way of following skiers.
● When setting off, have a good look round first.

# Walking on skis

Ski walking using skis and poles is simple enough on flat ground. Get into a relaxed stance with your knees bent and hips forward, with both skis parallel, a short distance apart, and flat on the ground. Hold your ski poles upright in each hand and plant them in the snow. Get used to the feel of the skis by sliding them back and fore, jumping with them, and lifting them one at a time.

If the ground is completely flat, push off with the right pole as you slide your right ski forward, and build up an easy rhythm moving left leg and left pole, then right leg and right pole, and so on. If you are on a slight downhill slope, you can push with both poles together, crouching down and propelling the skis forward. If you go uphill you have to learn the **herringbone** or **sidestep** technique.

## Safety first

● Make sure your boots fit properly, and that the bindings are properly adjusted. If you don't make the right preparation before you start you can hurt yourself.
● Avoid walking on the piste itself. If you must walk, stick to the side of the piste out of other skiers' way.
● If there is an accident, stop and give help if you can. Make sure the rescue services are told immediately. In most ski resorts they use either helicopters, or rescuers who can ski a stretcher down the slope.

## Sidestep

The sidestep is used to walk up a steep slope. The skis must be across the fall line, with their uphill edges pressed into the snow to prevent **sideslip**.

## Herringbone

The herringbone is a faster way to go up a gentle slope. The skis are angled so the inside edges press into the snow. The poles are used to push behind.

## Falling down

## Getting up

You're unlikely to learn to ski without falling. When you do fall, sit down to one side. Never sit on your skis or you'll slide downhill.

First check that you're all right. Move your skis side-on to the fall line, and push yourself up with one or both ski poles.

# Turning round

## Star turn

The easiest type of turn on flat ground is the **star turn**. Turn around by moving your skis like the hands of a clock while facing outwards. Use your poles to keep your balance, being careful not to take too big steps or cross over the ski tails. This would lead to overbalancing.

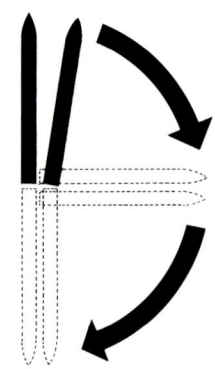

## Herringbone turns

The herringbone turn method can be used to turn round on a steeper slope when you need to change to the sidestep. You face uphill while turning, using a similar movement to the star turn. Prevent yourself from slipping back by pushing your ski poles firmly into the snow behind you.

## Kick turn

The **kick turn** is a fast and fancy way of turning on a slope. You start with your skis across the fall line, supporting your weight on your ski poles. To turn, first kick the downhill ski vertical. Then rotate it through an arc, keeping the tail in the snow. When it's lying alongside the other ski, but pointing in the opposite direction, you step round with the uphill ski.

In the kick turn, first balance with your ski poles and then kick one ski vertical.

Keep the tail in the snow, while letting the nose fall downwards to lie alongside the other ski.

To face in the right direction, step round the other ski. Use ski poles for support.

# Skiing downhill

Skiing straight downhill, which is called a **schuss**, is easy on a gentle slope. On steeper slopes though, it can become uncontrollably fast and scary. This is why skiers usually zig-zag downhill from side to side.

The ski boots force you into the correct stance with your knees bent and your body forwards. Look ahead and not down at the tips of your skis. Hold your ski poles at a 45 degree angle behind you. As you go faster you can crouch down and lean further forward to keep your balance. You can absorb any bumps in the snow using your legs as shock absorbers. The fastest position for high speed skiing is the **egg position**, used by racers for minimum wind resistance.

To turn toward the fall line without sliding out of control plant your poles in the snow ahead of you as shown on the right. Then walk your skis around until you face downhill.

# The snowplough

If you are skiing straight downhill, rather than zig-zagging across the slope, the only way to regulate your speed is to use the **snowplough**. This can bring you to a complete halt on gentle slopes.

The basic snowplough position is a wide vee, with the tips of the skis close together and the tails as far apart as possible. To get to this position you have to bend your knees inwards with your legs apart. Angle the skis so that the inner edges bite into the snow with equal pressure. It's not a comfortable position, and is hard work to keep up for more than a few minutes. The wider you can make the snowplough the slower you will go.

Skier faces down the fall line with upper body relaxed.

Knees push inwards.

Skis are angled to form a wedge against the snow.

# How to turn

The upper body faces downhill, away from the turn.

The ski is wedged and weighted to control the turn.

When you are skiing downhill in the snowplough position, you can turn across the fall line by putting your weight onto one ski. In the picture above, the skier has shifted his weight onto the right ski, angling it and pushing it against the snow. This will make him turn to the left. The left ski should slide round to keep pace with the right ski which does the steering. Notice how his upper body is turned towards the right ski, with his weight over it, while his knee and foot control the steering. You need to resist the natural impulse to lean into the turn, as you would do with cycling, and you should always face down the hill. To turn to the left you put your weight onto the left ski.

## Getting it right

At first it's difficult to get the hang of leaning your body out of the turn, which is necessary for smooth turning. A good exercise is to touch your outside downhill knee with your inside uphill hand in mid turn. This keeps your upper body turned downhill and facing away from the turn.

Doing the snowplough incorrectly can lead to problems like doing the splits or getting your skis crossed. Both are caused by edging your skis into the snow incorrectly. Practice will help you to do these turns.

23

# The ski lift

Once you can do the snowplough and the snowplough turns, you're ready to move on to steeper slopes. To get to these you use ski lifts. All resorts have an assortment of lifts serving their pistes. To use them you have to buy a **Ski Pass** which allows you to use all the lifts in the area.

The main lifts of the resort carry large numbers of people to the various ski areas. These are usually either gondolas or **funicular railways**. The funicular travels on rails up the mountainside, while the more modern gondola or **bubble lift** is suspended on cables high above the ground. Both work on a cunning system whereby the gondola or funicular going down pulls the one going up. Although they go very high and carry thousands of people, accidents are rare.

## Open or closed

All resorts have signs up showing which lifts are open, usually marked in green. Closed lifts are shown in red. They are closed if there is not enough snow or if the weather is poor. For instance, high winds can make elevated lifts dangerous. If there is poor visibility caused by a snow storm, or the risk of an **avalanche,** the ski lifts will be stopped.

Some lifts may develop big queues. Queue patiently. Better still, get up early, or find the lifts without queues.

# Chair lifts and drag lifts

Other lifts which service the pistes are **chair lifts** and **drag lifts**. Chair lifts hang from a cable which moves continuously above the ground. These let you sit down and enjoy a mid air ride with your skis on. Each chair usually takes two people, though some are designed for four. Their main disadvantage is that in an icy wind it can be a very cold way to travel as you sit there unprotected.

To get on a chair lift, move into position in front of the chair, hold your ski poles in one hand, and watch the chair as it approaches. Catch it with your free hand and sit down. Lower the safety bar and keep your skis pointing upwards. At the top there is a ramp for you to launch yourself off from the chair. Push yourself off as you reach the lip of this ramp, and ski down it.

T-bar lifts drag you up the slope as if you were on water skis. You wait in line for an attendant to put the T-bar under your backside. Be prepared for the sudden pull as it starts to drag you up the hill. Don't lean backwards or try to sit down. You can travel on a T-bar alone, or with another person. As long as he or she is reasonably capable it's not a difficult ride. You do have to keep your skis together and make sure that they don't cross. Another kind of drag lift is the **poma** or **button drag lift.** This drags skiers up the hill one at a time, and is generally reckoned to be easier to use than the T-bar.

To use the **T-bar drag lift** you need some skill, particularly on a steep slope.

# Traversing

In downhill skiing you go either straight down the fall line of the hills or you ski across them using the traverse or the sideslip technique to reduce your downhill speed. The left hand figure in the photograph is doing the classic schuss, blasting down at full speed. The figure on the right of the photograph is making a real mess of a traverse, and is about to end up in a pile of snow! His body is leaning into the hill rather than over his skis. This is making them slip away from under him as he heads off out of control down the hill. Compare his body angle with the illustration on the right which shows the correct position. The uphill shoulder is bent forward and the skier is looking down the hill. The hips are pressed into the hillside.

## Why go across?

Traversing is skiing across a hill at a controlled speed, rather than skiing flat-out direct down the fall line. The traverse can be used with linked turns to zig-zag your way down a steep hill, regulating speed by the steepness of the descent which can be adjusted by turning the skis up or downhill. Keep your skis parallel, except when you use the snowplough movement to make the necessary downhill turns. Even at a slight downhill angle you can ski quite fast. If you want to come to a complete stop, push out the back of the downhill ski and allow your skis to side-slip to a halt.

# The right technique

To traverse across a hillside the skis must be angled at the edge so that they have some grip on the snow. If the skis are flat, they will sideslip down the fall line.

To angle your skis correctly you must push your hips and knees into the hillside, while your upper body leans out so that you don't overbalance. Your body is bent like a banana with your upper body bending out and your lower body bending in. This keeps you balanced and allows you to push straight down onto your skis. The edges of the skis push into the snow. You must always have more weight on your downhill ski. If you do this you will be leaning out away from the hill correctly. You should remember to look downhill.

## Body position

Traversing is simple to learn so long as you take up the right body position. If your upper body leans too far into the hill, your skis won't grip and will slide away from under you. If your lower body isn't pushed into the hill, your skis will be too flat on the snow and will sideslip down the hill. The instructor in the photo is showing excellent traverse technique.

# Sideslipping

Sideslipping is not always a mistake. Allowing the skis to slide on the snow is useful in various ways such as for parallel turning, without using the snowplough. It is easiest to learn on the hard packed snow of the piste, but is very difficult on loose, powder snow.

To sideslip you use the traverse body position, but the skis are kept flat on the snow and allowed to slip down the hill. This means that you can go directly down a hill at a controlled speed, rather than going back and forwards across it using traverses linked by turns. It is a useful technique for getting down a narrow run where there is not enough room to make turns, or where it's too steep to risk a schuss straight down the fall line. It can be used if you want to drop a little way down the hillside while traversing, and also to stop quickly.

## Slipping at an angle

You can sideslip forwards, backwards and sideways down a hill. If your skis are completely side-on to the fall line, they will slide most slowly. When you want to stop, you gently edge them into the snow by pushing your knees into the hillside until you come to a standstill. If you sideslip with your skis pointing down the hill, you will go faster. The more they point down the hill, the faster you will go until you are no longer sideslipping but are on a schuss straight down the fall line. Sideslipping so that your skis face slightly uphill can also be used to stop quickly from a fast traverse.

# Sideslip technique

For the sideslip you start with your body facing downhill in the banana position just like the traverse, with skis side-on to the hill. You flatten your skis by pushing them downhill which will release their edge grip on the snow. Sometimes it's easiest to get them moving by pushing out the downhill ski first, and then moving the uphill ski parallel to it. Notice how the skier in the photograph looks where she is going, and the comparative steepness of the slope which can be descended without traversing or skiing straight downhill.

# Weight control

Throughout the sideslip most of your weight will be on the downhill ski. If you lean forwards the front of the skis will begin to head down the hill leading to a forward sideslip, while if you lean backwards the tails of the skis will head down the hill leading to a backwards sideslip. Controlling sideslip needs plenty of practice, but once you can do it, it is a great sensation and leads on to much faster skiing.

29

# Faster turns

If you go to a popular ski resort you will see all kinds of turns being used as the skiers zig-zag down the hills. The least experienced skiers will be using the basic snowplough turn, described on page 22. It is slow but reliable.

The better skiers will use faster forms of the snowplough, not opening the tails of their skis so wide to begin the turn, and bringing them parallel again as soon as possible to increase their speed. The fastest skiers won't use the snowplough at all. They will rely on parallel turns, using technique and speed to sideslip their skis from side to side across the fall line. The final category of turn is the **carved turn**. This is a really difficult technique only used by top professional **slalom** racers to help them win races.

## Why go parallel?

In a parallel turn, the skis stay parallel throughout the change of direction. This is initiated by a combination of the correct body movements and speed. The result is that parallel turns are neater, quicker, look better, and require less effort than snowplough turns. With commitment and practice parallel turning can be mastered quite quickly, but the snowplough and all its variations must be mastered first. It is used not only when you are learning, but by experts to make safe turns in difficult conditions.

# The linked snowplough

In the basic snowplough the skis stay open in a wedge throughout the turn. The better control you have of the snowplough, the more time you will spend with your skis parallel between turns.

To move from the basic snowplough into a traverse more quickly, the skis can be allowed to sideslip parallel as soon as the turn is complete but before the snowplough is finished. Then when you are ready to turn again, you open the skis wide for the next snowplough.

# Turning at speed

The object of the advanced snowplough turn is to be able to start from a fairly steep traverse, with your skis only pushed out into a small wedge. A much narrower snowplough is all that is needed to turn at speed. It is only held for a second until you are facing downhill. You then slide your skis parallel, pushing your knees hard into the turn so that they sideslip into the next traverse. Planting your inside pole in the snow helps to put your weight onto the new downhill ski as you go parallel.

# Moguls and hotdogging

A special turn is used for moguls. It is done on the top of the bumps which is the easiest place for the skis to **pivot**. You sit down, to lower your centre of gravity, with both poles supporting you, and spin your skis to face in the new direction. Then you stand up as you ski down into the next dip.

Coping with **moguls** is an advanced technique, but every skier comes across them on the steepest slopes. Moguls are lumps and bumps made by other skiers carving tight turns in the snow. They can't be flattened by the piste machines, and as the season wears on they get worse. They make for a rough passage and demand very fast reactions.

Mogul skiing can be so tricky that there is a special competition called **hotdogging**. This involves skiing down a mogul-course of around 300 metres, with points awarded for speed, turns, jumps and overall control. Falls bring penalty points. It's a spectacular competition to watch, and the spills are all part of the fun.

# Jumping with skis

It is not difficult to become airborne with skis. If you hit a mogul or ridge at speed, this will happen automatically. In some cases it may be necessary, such as to avoid a snow-covered low lying object when skiing at speed.

The basic technique for a good jump is to flex your knees as you hit your take-off ramp or ridge. You can then straighten your legs to push off as you go into the air. During the mid air part of the jump you tuck up with your knees pulled up under you. Keep your ski tips pointing slightly down, with the skis parallel to one another and also parallel to the landing slope which should have a long **run-out**. Just before landing straighten your legs, but let them flex to take the shock as your skis hit the snow. Ski jumping like this is an exciting pastime.

## Pre-jumping

Pre-jumping is a technique used by downhill competition racers to cut down their time in the air. Being in the air is always slower than being on the ground. Pre-jumping needs perfect timing. You jump just before the bump or lump, tucking up your legs so that your skis just clear it rather than take off from it. You then stretch your legs to get your skis back down on the snow as soon as possible. By doing this you avoid making unwanted jumps when skiing. The skier in the photograph above shows off perfect pre-jumping technique, finding his way to the bottom of the course as fast as possible in a major downhill racing competition.

# Skiing in powder snow

Powder snow is fresh snow which hasn't been compacted, either by the piste machine or other skiers. At its best it has a light, dry, fluffy quality very unlike the hard packed, icy snow usually found on the piste. You can ski through powder snow up to your knees, though it obviously slows you down. It can be unnerving skiing without being able to see your skis. The deeper the powder the more difficult powder skiing becomes. The basic techniques are the same, but you weight both skis equally and tend to ski more down the fall line to keep up speed. You also lean back a little so that your skis don't plough into the snow.

# Off piste

Some people liken skiing on piste to skiing on roads. They look to off piste skiing to get them away from all that. You have to go off piste to find the best virgin powder snow, but there are many more difficulties and dangers in this kind of skiing.

The first stage in off piste skiing is to get used to unprepared snow conditions. You can do this by venturing to the sides of the piste where this is possible. The technical skills you need are not much greater than for skiing on piste. Once you leave the piste though, you need to know about mountains and weather conditions, and the further afield you go the more knowledge you need. It is not for beginners to try. In some resorts well used off piste routes can be reached by the main ski lift networks. In others you may have to walk to the start of your ski area.

## Top places

In Europe the Vallée Blanche of Chamonix below Mont Blanc is reckoned to be the longest and most scenic off piste run in the world. Nearby, Verbier in Switzerland has off piste routes well served by its ski lifts. To the south, Val-d'Isère in France has a good reputation for off piste skiing, though it does have avalanches. St Anton in Austria also offers good off piste conditions. Among the American resorts Vail, and Breckenridge, both in Colorado, have good off piste routes.

# Safety off piste

Heading away from the safety of the piste signs, near Murren in the Swiss Alps.

There are many dangers in off piste skiing. They include getting lost, falling down a crevasse, or getting buried by an avalanche. You may also come across difficult conditions, such as breakable **crust snow** which gives way under your weight, or heavy, wet snow which twists your legs in a fall. Both can lead to accidents when you are many miles from any help.

● Use safety straps to attach your skis to your boots. If they come off in a fall, it can be very hard to find them.

● Never ski alone. Unless you really know what you are doing and are confident of your navigation, always ski with a qualified guide.

● Ski safely and take no unnecessary risks. Carry an **avalanche transmitter** if possible.

## Avalanches

An avalanche is a mass of snow that slides down the mountainside. It buries anything in its way. Every few years a number of people die in avalanches. The snow slides because the top layer is not properly stuck to the bottom layer. Avalanches are mostly a danger off piste. On piste areas, if an avalanche threatens, a resort will post danger signs and will normally close the runs by shutting down lifts. If weather conditions allow it, experts may dynamite the snow to create a controlled avalanche. You must be fully aware of potential avalanche danger when going off piste.

# Ski safaris and touring

There are several variations on off piste skiing. Ski safaris are organized holidays in which a qualified guide leads a party on a variety of off piste trails each day.

Heli skiing is an expensive way to reach the most inaccessible off piste runs, hiring both helicopter and guide to take you to the starting point and to make sure you get safely home. The most popular area for this is the Canadian Rockies of North America.

Ski touring is a pure form of skiing, in which the ski party is led on a tour. The trip may last several days. Members climb uphill carrying all their equipment, camp in Alpine huts or tents, and ski downhill.

# Cross-country skiing

**Cross-country** skiing or **langlauf** involves skiing along prepared cross-country trails with gentle ups and downs. It is looked at as a different sport from Alpine downhill skiing. Special long skis are used and boots are designed to lift at the heels to allow you to slide the skis forward in a steady rhythm.

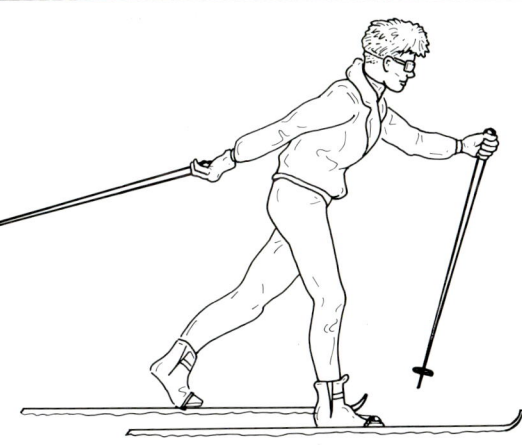

# Competition

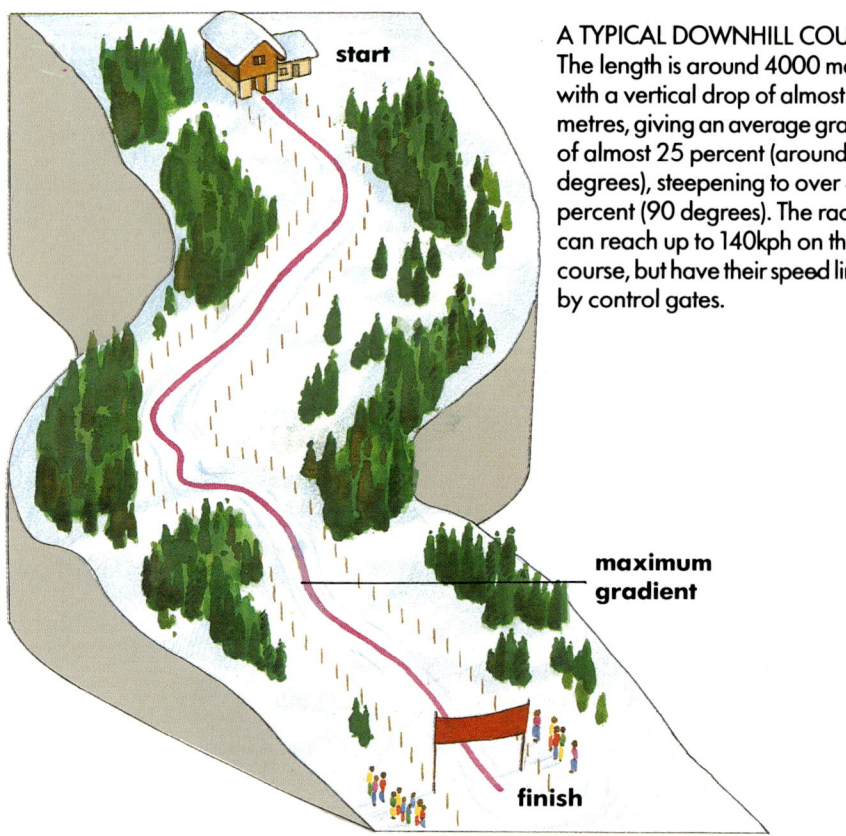

start

**A TYPICAL DOWNHILL COURSE**
The length is around 4000 metres with a vertical drop of almost 1000 metres, giving an average gradient of almost 25 percent (around 15 degrees), steepening to over 40 percent (90 degrees). The racers can reach up to 140kph on the course, but have their speed limited by control gates.

maximum gradient

finish

The three main types of ski competition are Special Slalom, Giant Slalom and Downhill Racing, for both men and women, though the women ski on less demanding courses. The Winter Olympics are held every four years. The World Ski Championships, which use these same three competitions, are also held every four years. They are staggered with the Olympics so that there is a major single-resort event every second year.

The World Cup is an annual points series made up of a dozen or so events. Racing is held in Europe, the US, New Zealand and Japan. The most important resorts are Sestriere and Val Gardena in Italy, Val-d'Isère and Valloire in France, Kitzbühel and Saalbach in Austria, Wengen and Adelboden in Switzerland, and Aspen and Waterville Valley in the US. Most top racers are classed as amateurs, but the best are heavily sponsored and earn large amounts of money. Two of the most famous racers in the history of ski competition are Jean Claude Killy and Ingemar Stenmark.

# Downhill racing

Downhill racing is the fastest and most dangerous event of all. It has a high accident rate. The racing rules state that the course must have a maximum vertical drop of 800-1000 metres, with a 'best descent' time of two minutes or less. Competitors use the crouched egg position whenever they can, pre-jumping bumps and using a higher crouch to allow steering. They wear specially prepared skis up to 230cm long. Crash helmets are compulsory.

## Special Slalom

Sir Arnold Lunn drew up the rules for the first Alpine slalom races in 1928. The event is now called Special Slalom, and is a test of agility and control. Two courses are set on a short, steep (20-27 degrees) hillside. The rules state that competitors have to ski through a maximum course of 55-75 gates set 4-5 metres apart, in a vertical drop of 180-220 metres. The poles which form the gates may be toppled, but a competitor missing a gate is disqualified.

# Giant Slalom

The Giant Slalom started in 1934 as a way of cutting down the speed of downhill racing. It became an Olympic sport in 1952. It combines the speed of downhill racing with the turning skills of Special Slalom, but has become so specialized that few ski racers are able to win both Giant Slalom and the other types of competition. The skill is to turn through the gates losing as little speed as possible, by taking the shortest and fastest line and speeding up out of the gates as quickly as possible.

Giant Slalom has gates set wider apart than Special Slalom. The course of about 1500 metres is longer, and there is a vertical drop of 300-400 metres for men, reduced to 300-350 metres for women. The course takes around 90 seconds to complete.

## Other slalom events

Giant Slalom and Special Slalom are highly specialized. Simpler competitions for local events include:
● Single Pole Slalom which allows slalom racers to ski round single poles rather than through gates.
● Dual Slalom, a parallel competition in which two short slalom courses are set alongside one another, with exactly the same gates. Two racers start together at the top of each course. The one who gets to the bottom first wins. They then change courses, with the best overall time winning.

# The big jump

Ski jumping is another highly specialized competition. The competitors launch and take off from specially-built ski jump ramps, using special long skis and no poles. The results are based on the distance of the jump from take-off to landing. At the jump at Planica in Yugoslavia, Piotr Fijas of Poland set a World Record of 194 metres in 1987. Tina Lehtola of Finland set a women's record of 110 metres at Ruka in Finland in 1981.

The four stages of the jump are: the run-in, when the jumper goes steeply down the ramp to build up maximum speed; the take-off, when he or she hits the end of the ramp as it levels out; the flight, during which the jumper leans forward over the skis and for which he or she is also marked on style; and the landing and final run-out.

# The Flying K

The Flying Kilometre is the greatest test of speed. It is highly specialized and very dangerous. It takes place on a few special courses throughout the skiing world, such as the course at Les Arcs in France shown in the photo. In 1988 Michael Prufer of Monaco set a World Speed Record of 223.741kph (139.030mph) here, while Tarja Mulari of Finland set a women's record of 214.413kph (133.234mph). The course is around two kilometres long. It starts gently, then gets steeper down a perfectly prepared 40-45 degree slope. Here the skier's speed is recorded over one kilometre. At the end of the course there is a run-out section where the skier goes uphill to lose speed.

# *Snowboarding*

Snowboards are good for aerial tricks and other forms of freestyle.

If you visit any ski resort nowadays you will see **snowboards.** Some of the older, more traditional skiers do not like them, but they do not get in the way on the ski slopes, and they definitely appeal to young people. Snowboards first began to appear in the early 1980s, and are based on surfboards. The great difference between snowboarding and skiing is that you stand sideways on, using standard ski boots or special snowboard boots in modified bindings, with one foot leading. You can sideslip, traverse, or schuss straight down the hill at high speed, carving and skidding turns as you slide over the snow. You use your back foot to steer. Your weight is over the front foot as the back foot is used to swing the tail of the board from side to side, with speed giving stability.

With a snowboard exciting aerial manoeuvres can soon be added to the repertory.

## Design helps

On a snowboard, the length of the steel edges in contact with the snow controls the stability. As with skiing heavy riders need longer snowboards than light riders. Wider boards are better in soft snow, but narrow boards can be turned faster and are quickest on hard packed snow. The sidecut is more obvious than on skis. The deeper the sidecut, the more an experienced rider can carve turns without sideslip. The squarish tails are rounded to make the most of what snowboarders call swingweight – the weight on your back foot needed to turn the board. There is also a lot of design hype to wade through!

typical length: 150cms

construction:
laminated wood
and fibreglass
with steel edges

sidecut helps
turning

# World ski resorts

## IN EUROPE

The Alpine countries are best known for European skiing, though the Cairngorms of Scotland and parts of Scandinavia are also popular.

In Switzerland we find many traditional resorts across the Bernese Oberland and the Valais area. Famous names such as Gstaad, Crans/Montana (two linked villages), Saas Fee, Verbier, and Zermatt are part of this region. Zermatt has the country's highest skiing going up to 3,810 metres. In the east the best known resorts include St Moritz, popular with the very rich, and Davos/Klosters.

Skiing has a similarly long tradition in Austria, though the mainly lower resorts can suffer from a shorter ski season. Famous names

Above: Les Arcs, one of the modern style of French, purpose built Alpine ski resorts.

include Kitzbühel, Lech, Zurs, Solden and Obergurgl/Hochgurgl. The last two resorts are high and help to extend the Austrian season. In France there is skiing in the Pyrenees in the south, but much more in the Alps in the east. Here there are many big modern purpose-built resorts. Among the best known are the twin resorts of Val-d'Isère/Tignes which have a huge skiing area dubbed L'Espace Killy, and Courcheval, Meribel and Val Thorens which are linked to form Les Trois Vallées.

Italy's skiing takes place in the Alps and Dolomites, with Cervinia and Courmayeur allowing skiing across the Swiss and French borders.

## NORTH AMERICA, JAPAN AND THE SOUTHERN HEMISPHERE

In recent years the Rocky Mountains of the US and Canada have had a better snow season than Europe. Among the best known centres are Aspen, Breckenridge and Vail in Colorado. Also well known are the linked resorts of Heavenly Valley, which is the largest ski area in North America, and Squaw Valley, site of the 1960 Winter Olympics, in the Lake Tahoe area on the Nevada/California border. In New Mexico to the south the Taos Ski Valley has skiing up to 3600 metres. On the east coast the American Appalachian and Canadian Laurentian Mountains provide a large skiing area north of New York. This includes Lake Placid where both the 1932 and 1980 Winter Olympics were held.

Japan is also a land of keen skiers, though the slopes can be very crowded. The 1972 Winter Olympics were held at Sapporo in the north. Most of the other resorts are in the centre of the country on the slopes of Japan's dormant volcanoes.

In the southern hemisphere the skiing season starts around June and ends around September. The Southern Alps of the South Island of New Zealand have good skiing although it is difficult to get to some of the ski slopes. In the North Island Whakapapa or Turoa in the Mount Ruapehu area mid-way between Wellington and Auckland are popular. In neighbouring Australia the Alpine area of New South Wales and Victoria, between Sydney and Melbourne, is best known. Good conditions can also be found in South America in Argentina, Bolivia, Brazil, Chile, Colombia and Uruguay.

Below: Dropping down into the US resort of Killington, Vermont.

# International associations

Australian Ski Federation,
Olympic Park, Swan Street,
Melbourne 3002, Victoria, Australia

Austria Ski Association,
Osterreichischer Skiverband,
Olympiastrasse 10, A-6020,
Innsbruck, Austria

British Association of Ski Instructors,
Grampian Road, Aviemore,
Inverness-shire PH221RL, UK

British Ski Federation,
258 Main Street, East Calder,
West Lothian EH53 0EE, UK

Canadian Ski Association,
1600 James Naismith Drive,
Gloucester, Ontario K1B 5N4,
Canada

French Ski Federation,
50 Rue des Marquisats, BP451,
F-74009 Annecy Cedex, France

Ski Association of Ireland,
Bridge House, Newcastle West,
Co Limerick Ireland

Italian Ski Federation,
Federazione Italiano Sport Invernali,
Via Piarnesi 44/b
I-20137 Milano, Italy

New Zealand Ski Association,
9th Floor, West Tower,
Education House,
178-182 Willis Street,
Wellington, New Zealand

Norwegian Ski Federation,
Norges Skiforbund,
Houger Skolevei 1, N-1351 Rud,
Norway

Spanish Ski Federation,
Federacion Espanola Deportes Da
Invierno, Claudio Coello,
32 29001 Madrid,
Spain

Swedish Ski Association,
Svenska Skidforbyundet,
Odrotlens Hus,
S-123 Farsta,
Stockholm, Sweden

Swiss Ski Federation,
Federation Suisse de Ski,
Worbstrasse 52, CH-3074,
Switzerland

United States Ski Association,
1500 Kearns Blvd, HWY 248,
PO Box 100, Park City UT84060, USA

# Glossary

**ABS:** a hard moulded plastic skin used in ski manufacture
**avalanche:** snow sliding in a mass down a mountainside

**avalanche transmitter:** a radio transmitter which sends a signal to help locate someone buried in an avalanche. Avalanche transmitters should be carried by off piste skiers.

**binding release system:** a quick release which separates the boot from the ski in a heavy fall. It is adjustable, to take into account the conditions, weight of the skier, and the type of skiing

**bubble lift:** a bubble lift or gondola has enclosed cabins on a continually moving wire to take skiers up the mountainside

**button drag lift:** a type of drag lift that pulls one skier at a time up the slope, using a rod with a round plate tucked between the legs

**camber:** the curve which is built into the bottom of a ski

**carved turn:** a turn made by banking a ski onto its side – a very advanced manoeuvre

**chair lift:** a lift that takes skiers up the slope on chairs suspended from an overhead cable

**cross-country skiing:** a route which can take the skier downhill, uphill, and along level ground, also called *langlauf* or Nordic skiing

**crust snow:** a hard surface frozen on the top of soft snow

**downhill skiing:** skiing down a slope, also known as Alpine skiing

**drag lift:** a lift which pulls you up a slope

**dry slope:** an artificial ski slope used mainly for practice

**egg position:** a position where the body is tucked into a ball for maximum aerodynamic efficiency downhill

**fall line:** the most direct way downhill

**funicular railway:** a railway which goes directly up the side of a mountain, with the weight of the carriage coming down balancing the carriage going up

**gondola lift:** another name for a bubble lift

**herringbone:** walking uphill with your skis in a wide vee

**hot dog:** freestyle tricks on skis

**kick turn:** the quickest way to turn right round on skis from a stationary position

**langlauf:** another name for cross-country skiing

**mogul:** lumps and bumps on the piste worn by the passage of many skis

**off piste:** skiing on snow away from the specially prepared piste areas

**on piste:** skiing on downhill areas that have been specially prepared and graded according to difficulty

**parallel turn:** sideslipping the skis to turn from one side to the other across the fall line.

**piste:** see on piste

**pivot:** turning your skis around a fixed spot

**poma:** another name for a button lift

**powder snow:** light, freshly fallen snow

**release mechanism lever:** the lever which releases the ski binding

**run-out:** an uphill slope used to lose speed at the end of a fast downhill run

**salopettes:** dungaree-style trousers designed for skiing

**schuss:** skiing straight downhill

**sidecut:** the amount a ski is cut in at the sides

**sideslip:** allowing skis to slip sideways down a slope

**sidestep:** stepping sideways with skis on

**Ski Evolutif:** a French teaching system starting with very short skis, and changing to slightly longer skis as you progress

**ski lift:** a mechanical means of getting up the slope

**Ski Pass:** a card which allows a skier to use all the lifts in the area. It is usually expensive

**ski stoppers:** when the binding on a ski is released, two small rods are pushed down into the snow to prevent the ski running away downhill. These are called ski stoppers

**slalom:** a ski competition which involves linked turns round a series of markers

**snow blindness:** loss of sight caused by the very bright snow. Suitable goggles or sunglasses should be worn

**snowboard:** an offshoot of the surfboard and skateboard which has now become very popular on ski slopes

**snowplough:** a wedge position used to slow down or promote a turn

**sous-pull:** a zippered, cotton shirt

**star turn:** turning round by taking big, wide steps with the front of the skis

**sun block:** a cream used to prevent sunburn

**T-bar drag lift:** a drag lift with a T-shape to pull two skiers up the slope

**traverse:** skiing across a slope

**virgin snow:** snow which has never been skied on before

# Index

The numbers in **bold** are illustrations

ABS 9, 46
Australia 45
Austria 4, 44
avalanches 35, 46

bindings 10, 11, **11**
binding release system 12, 46
boots 10, **10**, 11, **11**
bubble lift 24, 46
button drag lifts 25, 46
buying skis 9

camber 8, 47
Canada 45
carrying skis 12, **12**
carved turns 30, 47
chair lifts 25, 47
classes 5
clothing **4**, 6, **6**, 7, **7**, 12
cross-country skiing 37, **37**, 47
crust snow 36, 47

downhill racing **33**, 38, **38**, 39, **39**
downhill skiing 21, **21**, 47
drag lifts 25, **25**, 47
dry ski slopes 15, 47

egg position 21, 47

falling down 19, **19**, 26
fall line 12, 47
fast turns 30
filing ski edges 9
flying K 41, **41**
footwear 10
France 44
funicular railway 24, 47

getting up 19, **19**
giant slalom 38, 40, **40**
glare 7
gondola 12, 24, **24**, 47

heli skiing 37
herringbone 18, 19, **19**, 47
herringbone turn 20
hiring skis 9
hotdogging 32, 47

Italy 44

Japan 45
jumping **4**, 33, **33**, 41

kick turns 20, **20**, 47
kindergarten 14

langlauf 37, **37**, 47
lessons 14
linked snowplough 31

moguls 32, **32**, 47

North America 45
nursery slopes 5

on piste 5, 16, **16**, 47
off piste 5, 34, **34**, 35, **35**, 36, **36**, 37, **37**, 47
overtaking 17

parallel turns 17, 30, **30**, 31, 47
pioneers 4
piste 5, 16, **16**, 34, 47
pivot turns 32, **32**, 47
poma drag lifts 25, 47
powder snow 5, 34, **34**, 35, **35**, 47
pre-jumping 33, **33**
putting on skis 12

release mechanism lever for skis 12, 47
resorts 5, 14, 44, 45
rights of way 17
run out 33, 47

safety 6, 17, 18, 36
Scandinavia 44
schools 14, **14**

schuss 21, 47
seasons 4, 6
short skis 8, 15, **15**
sidecut 8, 47
sideslip 19, 26, 27, 28, **28**, 29, **29**, 47
sidestep 18, 19, **19**, 47
ski care 9, **9**
ski construction 9
ski design 8, **8**
Ski Evolutif 15, **15**, 47
ski height 8, **8**
ski lifts 4, 24, **24**, 25, **25**, 47
ski pass 24, 47
ski poles 13, **13**
ski safaris 37
skis 8, **8**, 10, **10**, 11, 12, **12**
ski stoppers 12, 47
slalom **13**, 38, 39, **39**, 40, **40**, 47
snow blindness 6, 47
snowboards 42, **42**, 43, **43**, 47
snowmobile 5
snowplough 22, **22**, 47
snowplough turns 23, **23**, 30, 31, **31**, 47
South America 45
star turns 20, **20**, 47
Swiss Ski School 14
Switzerland 4, 5, 44

T-bar drag lifts 25, **25**, 47
touring 37
traverse 17, 26, **26**, 27, **27**, 47
turning 20, 21, **21**, 23, 30, **30**, 31, **31**, 32, **32**

US 45

virgin snow 5, 34, 35, 47

waxing skis 9
walking 18, **18**, **37**
Winter Olympics 38
World Cup 38
World Championship 38